Celebrating Solitude

ALSO BY RACHEL ASTARTE PICCIONE

101 Better Sex Tips
The Bride of Manhattan
The Exchange

Celebrating Solitude

How to Discover and Honor
Your Highest Self

Rachel Astarte Piccione

Green Oracle Press

Cover photo: Paul J. Curley
Author photo: Chris Carroll

ISBN-10: 061571644X
ISBN-13: 978-0615716442

Printed in the United States of America.

This book is printed on acid-free paper.

*This book is dedicated to you,
the glorious spark of Source
that illuminates this life.*

CONTENTS

Married and Co-habitating Life

Solitude and Spirituality

All This is Yours

Introduction:
Entering the Temple of the Holy Self

Being solitary is being alone well: being alone luxuriously immersed in doings of your own choice, aware of the fullness of your own presence rather than of the absence of others.
—Alice Köller

In 2001, my father—a well-respected poet, professor, and renowned lover of solitude—died of liver cancer. Shortly thereafter, a long-term relationship that I'd always assumed would one day result in marriage, instead ended. Now in my thirties, I had to find a new place to live in the expensive expanse of New York City and create a whole new life for myself that did not include the wise counsel of my father or the comfort of a male companion. Sure, I had friends, but most of them were either busy living their own lives or lived in different cities. The same applied to my mother and two sisters. I felt more alone than I'd ever been in my entire life.

I threw myself into self-improvement by becoming active in international peace work. I became an ordained clergy member, selecting for myself the title of Peace Counselor. From there, I launched a Middle East peace organization, which employed the arts as a method of non-violent conflict resolution. I stood vigil every week in Union Square with Women in Black (Jews against the Occupation of Palestine), and later that year was asked to join their board. I gave readings at THAW (Theaters Against War) town hall meetings, and spoke at New York's New School on the topic of arts and peace. I wrote two novels, two screenplays, self-published a chapbook of poems, and traveled to India twice.

I got out there, lived fully, committed myself to what I thought was doing good in the world, but nearly every night I came home alone. And it bothered me.

Five years later, nearing forty, I had managed to survive living in the wild vitality of New York, but had nothing to show for my romantic life other than a few lovers-turned-email-pals. I decided to start fresh and embarked on a period of sexual abstinence, vowing that the next man with whom I shared my body would be my future husband. I felt charged, alive, and deliciously vivacious in my newfound self-possession. But a third, extended trip to India reinforced my worst fears. I was seen distinctly differently than I saw myself. As an unmarried thirty-something, I was treated as though I were used up, sexless. A woman physiologically, but romantically? At my age, I was considered as viable a mate as any of the sacred cows that ambled along the dusty roads. When I returned to the States, I had to face the fact that I might very well live alone for the rest of my life. I knew I needed to make peace with this revelation.

But how?

Drawing on the skills I learned as an independent child raised by parents who themselves were very strong individuals, I took a look at my current life in detail: character by character, belief by belief, habit by habit. I began to assess what kept me excited about getting out of bed in the morning. I came to realize how much, despite my occasional whining, I cherished my solitude. Yet, I saw so many women and men around me who were out there dating—not solely for the fun of meeting new people, but to find a mate. Someone, *anyone* (almost) who would deliver them from impending spinsterhood or eternal Peter Panesque bachelordom. Why, I wondered, did we need validation from society (in the form of a stable relationship) in order to be considered whole?

When I eventually married, my thoughts about solitude turned to other married people I knew and those living with partners. I saw so many couples leaning against each other, working to morph each of their individual psyches into one new one and present a unified front to the world. Were they finding peace in their lives as individuals? Or were they defining themselves in part or in whole by their role of Partner? It appeared more often than not to be the latter.

This led me to wonder how many other roles we play in life. What happens to the distinct and vital soul of each individual human being if we lose ourselves in each other—in our roles at work, in our famlies, to our friends, or in society as a whole? When I began working as a clinical hypnotherapist, the majority of my clients came to me feeling burned out and "stuck" in their lives. They were out of synch with themselves, having gotten caught up in diligently fulfilling their responsibilities to others—at home, in school, at work, and within the community.

Over time, it became clear to me that many of us have lost touch with the beauty of the Self and its innate sacred energy. It's what many refer to as our "highest self." I began to refer to this highest self as the Holy Self. Because we come from Source—God/Goddess, the Great Mystery, The Universe, or whatever name you choose to give it—we, too, carry Source within us. While it is true that we are all connected to each other, it is equally true that we are also connected to the Divine. There is great power in each of us, ingrained in us by Creation. That's powerful stuff. We need to honor that power in order to live the fullest life we can.

What I hope for this book is to share what solitude really means, what it can mean, and what we can look forward to when we embrace time with ourselves. Solitude is not a retreat from the world, but rather a way to recharge our energies—our Holy Selves—for the world. In doing so, we can become emotionally healthier and more spiritually accomplished—with or without a partner. So, find a quiet spot, close the door, turn the page, and start celebrating.

What is Solitude (and Why Should We Celebrate it)?

I have to be alone very often. I'd be quite happy if I spent from Saturday night until Monday morning alone in my apartment. That's how I refuel.
—Audrey Hepburn

What does solitude mean to you? A quiet room with a hot cup of tea? Silence at the end of a day's chores? A cabin in the woods? Peace and relaxation? Isolation and loneliness? We each come to the idea of solitude with a very personal definition, based on our life-long experiences with it—or without it. For some, solitude is to be avoided because it fills our hearts with sadness and a sense of abandonment. Perhaps it brings to mind the forced solitude of being punished and sent to our room as a child. For others, solitude is a welcome respite from the manic busyness of the day. A few of us may even fall somewhere in between these two feelings.

Healthful solitude is the time you set aside for yourself in order to perform whatever acts give you pleasure—reading, sketching, meditating, dancing, or taking a walk, for example. Based on that definition alone, most of us would agree that regular stints of aloneness help clear our minds. However, taking solitary time for yourself has another immense benefit. It's an opportunity to recharge your soul's batteries. These two concepts lead us to the ultimate goal, which is to rediscover the best, highest self you can be. I say "rediscover" because there was once a time when we were intimately connected to our highest selves: at birth. Even before. Prior to donning the roles and personas we needed to costume ourselves with in order to give our grand performance as human beings on a discriminating cultural stage, we were connected to the perfection of creative energy. That connection was as effortless as a drop of water joining the ocean. Solitude gives us time to refamiliarize ourselves with the innate spark of Source we carry within us.

So, besides reconnecting with the Divine, why should we bother carving out time for ourselves, recharging our batteries, etc.? Regular stints of solitude lead us to

> **Solitude is a gift you give yourself every day.**

live more peaceful lives internally *as well as* externally. If you grant yourself the permission to relish a few moments just for you, you will feel better. The benefits don't end there. Your cherished time alone, as if by magic, replenishes your resources to give back to others more fluidly and profoundly. In short, when you honor your self by taking time to reconnect with your soul and celebrate your very life, not only will your life become richer, that richness will, in turn, spill over into your lives with friends, family, colleagues...even strangers.

THE SOLITUDE EQUATION:

Taking time for yourself
+
Recharging your soul's batteries
=
Your Holy Self (The Best You You Can Be)

You may be thinking, *That sounds great, but I have a job/family/friends who need me a lot. Isn't spending time alone selfish?* Here's a fact: If you don't care for yourself—physically and emotionally—your energy gets depleted, just like a battery. Ever try to talk on your cellphone with no juice? Not very effective, right? Taking regular time for yourself allows you to recharge your batteries so you can give your most powerful energy to others *as well as yourself.* There's nothing selfish about that.

Don't think you have time? How about two minutes? Even the busiest parent or CEO has 120 seconds to spare. Of course, there will be times you'll want to devote more time to your Self, and you should. Developing a regular solitude practice helps you to develop your strengths, rejuvenate your soul—and have fun doing it. If you're still not convinced, think of it this way: Solitude is a gift you give yourself—and your loved ones—every day.

Defining Solitude

Take a sheet of paper and write the word SOLITUDE at the top. Without thinking, quickly jot down a list of words that come to mind when you hear/read the word "solitude." Keep going as long as you can. Don't be afraid to write non-sensical words or words that don't seem to fit. You'd be surprised by how the brain works; all your answers will give you some level of insight.

Once you're finished with your list, read through it and add up how many words feel positive, how many feel negative, and how many seem neutral.

For example:

> Journey
>
> Excitement
>
> Ginger tea
>
> Apprehension
>
> Darkness
>
> Quiet
>
> Incense
>
> Isolation
>
> Peacefulness

With this list, you can see that at least three of these words/phrases could be considered negative (Apprehension, Darkness, Isolation), while the others like Excitement, Quiet, and Peacefulness would probably be considered positive. Journey might be a neutral word, as might Incense (unless, of course, you're allergic to it). You get the idea. Only you know how you feel about each word or phrase.

Now note what the majority of your thoughts

are—negative, positive, or neutral. This will give you an indication of how to use this book to create a solitude practice that is exciting and effective for you. Regardless of where you fall in the spectrum of feelings about aloneness, keep in mind that this entire book was written for *you*, to help you be the best human being you can be.

Honoring the Holy Self

The kingdom of God is within you.
—Jesus

When we ask ourselves, *What is holy?*, saints, deities, sacred structures, and relics often come to mind. Being holy implies an anointing into perfection by the Great Creator, whomever He or She or It might be. But as 20th century Indian mystic Osho points out in *The Book of Understanding*, "Being is already as it should be, it is perfect. Nothing needs to be added to it, nothing can be added to it. It's a creation of existence. It comes out of perfection, hence it is perfect." Osho is not the only one who believes this. Other spiritual belief systems including Buddhism, Christianity, Hinduism, Animism, Jainism, Sufism, Paganism, and more lean toward the same thought—that all living beings are Divine, or at the very least they carry elements of the Divine within them.

Therefore, by nature, we are Divine. Even when we mess up or do stupid things, they are natural parts of the process of living. And since all living things are holy, the trip-ups along the path are holy as well. What is required of us is that we remain fully open and receptive, like an explosive rhododendron waiting for pollen-hunting honeybees. Simply being true to ourselves means that we are letting the perfection of nature take its course. It doesn't get much holier than that.

So, what does this have to do with solitude? It's important to begin creating a solitude practice by honoring your Holy Self. This has nothing to do with ego. The message here is not to consider yourself superior or all-powerful. Rather, it is to acknowledge yourself as *one of many* holy things in existence. In doing so, you will afford yourself the privilege of being treated with care and love. In addition, honoring our Holy Self gives us great practice in honoring *other* holy selves.

> **Solitude is a path toward your truest self.**

Your solitude practice is a gift you present to yourself. Solitude is a path toward becoming closer to your truest self. Along the journey you may very well face fear, disappointment, ugliness, self-pity, or anger. Maybe all of those aspects of Self and more. But you will also come to experience great peace and playfulness in your life. By fully experiencing your aloneness, you will discover a level of self-knowledge and self-love that perhaps you never knew existed or never thought you deserved. Here's the secret that Creation wants you to know: It does exist. And you deserve it.

Discovering Your Holy Self

Find a quiet place where you feel warm and secure. This can be a bedroom, living room, meditation room, or even a bath. Lie down comfortably, in bed, on the floor, or in your bath. Close your eyes and focus on your breath. As you breathe deeply, envision your body filling with light. To help this visualization along, you may wish to picture a large ball of bright white light above you, glowing and vibrating with positive energy. Once you have the image secure, imagine this great glowing ball sending its rays down to you.

With each inhalation, breathe in some of this light. As you exhale, force out any negative feelings you have about yourself. This includes criticisms about you by yourself or by others. Never mind if they're right. Let them go. They have no place or power here.

Begin to feel your body. This does not mean touch it. Instead, pay attention to the sensations fluttering under your skin. Imagine yourself radiating positive energy—the same energy that has transformed you right now from a stressed-out insecure person to another magical drop in the ocean of divine serenity. Remember that the positive energy you received and are now radiating originates from the same source. You are as holy as it is.

When you have spent a few minutes in this state—channeling divine energy, holding the power within you, and radiating it outward—open your eyes, and come slowly out of the meditation. Try to sustain this state as long as possible while you carry on with the rest of your day.

This exercise takes practice. Give yourself a gift of 5-10 minutes every day for at least a week to do this meditation. It's just a few minutes. If you're feeling stuck or not worthy, remember to be gentle with yourself; it took years to develop negative feelings. It takes time to unravel, honor, and release them.

Give and Take

Women need real moments of solitude and self-reflection to balance out how much of ourselves we give away.
—Barbara De Angelis

There is a natural concern that some of us will have about spending time alone on a regular basis: Being alone means being selfish. Women in particular suffer from this concern. Men do, too, but the nurturing nature of women makes it specifically hard to carve out that time we so desperately need without feeling we're letting down the people we love. How can we request solitude when there's a household to run? A family to care for? Friends who expect our availability at any moment? A boss who demands our top game every day?

> **Being alone ≠ Being selfish**

Look at it this way: Presumably, regardless of gender, you're not taking much time for yourself at the moment, yet the thought intrigues you enough that you have picked up this book. So. Your job is secure (for the time being), your house is clean and stocked with food, your family is cared for, your friends know they can call you any time of the day or night, and you—remarkably reliable you—will be there for them.

Gut check: Consult your second brain, the one that lives in your belly, or just above it, where your ribs meet the base of your sternum. How do you feel right now? You. The inside you. The Spark of Divinity you. How's your Holy Self doing? Chances are, that Holy Self is struggling to find a voice to answer this question. Or perhaps it's silent. Most likely, you're feeling drained and spread too thin.

If you continue this way, what do you think will happen? You'll keep giving and giving and eventually you'll begin to resent the very people you love and wish to help *because you have not taken care of your self*.

One of my hypnotherapy clients was a vibrant woman who worked for a humanitarian non-profit organization. She excelled at her job. She was a stellar wife and mother to a son who was doing well as a sophomore in college. She had scads of friends who loved her dearly. Regardless of how busy she was at work, she never turned down a project. When she came to see me and listed her accomplishments, she was on the verge of tears. I asked why. She told me she felt she had turned away from herself and the things she had once loved to do like dancing and making jewelry. While she was technically a good mother/colleague/friend, she was not being good to herself. The result was that she felt empty inside. When she gave to others, she was actually pulling energy out of a void within her.

Have you ever encountered someone who is incredibly giving but is clearly emotionally fried? Perhaps this person even wears the mask of perpetual exasperation over how—Happily! Happily!—busy she is just giving and doing and being there for everyone? When someone like that shines her blinding fluorescent light of assistance on you, how do you feel? Do you feel good about where that helpfulness is coming from? Probably not. Why? Because it's clear that this person has not given love to herself.

We can offer our energy to all the people we love, but we need to recharge our batteries on a regular basis or that energy will be drained. My client eventually took up jewelry-making again, using the time to recharge her soul's batteries. If she didn't, she'd have continued on the path of giving when there was nothing left to give. Trying to help others with no energy is like having a party and trying to fill everyone's glass with an empty pitcher.

Solitude fills our pitcher. Solitude recharges our batteries. There's nothing selfish about that. In fact, by taking time to refuel our souls, we can actually give *more* to those around us than if we just plow through, giving and giving even long after our soul's energy is depleted.

Why We Avoid Aloneness

What a lovely surprise to discover how unlonely being alone can be.
—Ellen Burstyn

Unfortunately, "to be alone" typically implies that one has no human company with whom to interact, or that one lacks the skills to socialize. To be alone can also imply the choice to isolate oneself, usually as a result of some negative event, such as an argument or a traumatic experience.

These associations cause many of us to avoid being alone. No one in his or her right mind would *want* to be alone, right? Unless of course you're Greta Garbo in *Grand Hotel* (the film in which she famously pleaded, "I *vant* to be alone."). Now, I admit I don't speak from experience on this topic. I've never shied away from being alone. Maybe it was my older sister's influence. She spent most of the time isolated in her room, listening to medieval recorder music, reading Tolkien, and burning Gonesh No. 6 incense. She also spent hours creating elaborate worlds with little glass animals. She gave the miniature dogs, horses, bears, and rabbits names and histories. She built them homes out of shoeboxes. I was so impressed that I took up the game as well.

After my glass animal obsession passed, I began making radio dramas with the cassette recorder I'd received one Christmas. Despite the fact that no one would ever hear the tapes but me, I worked painstakingly

> **It is not pointless to enjoy experiences like sunsets and home-cooked dinners alone. The very important person you're sharing with is yourself.**

to create solid productions with sound effects and numerous characters, including a precocious eight-year-old named Gwendolyn Bradley. It was surprising I chose to create a character who was my contemporary, considering that I despised kids my age. They were smelly, mean, and stupid. They pushed, yelled, and seemed to go out of their way to hurt one another.

Around this time, I came across a book called, *How to Be Your Own Best Friend* by Mildred Newman and Bernard Berkowitz. The prospect was alluring. Could I actually find fulfillment in myself without sticky interactions with unpredictable children my age? Would being my own best friend seem, well, weird? Without that book as a primer, I'm not sure I would have learned that alone time is essential to growth as a person.

Conversely, another of my clients sorely dislikes being alone. He's a master of socialization, befriending strangers on commuter trains and in bars faster than you can say Joey Tribiani's catch phrase on *Friends*. For him, submerging himself in other people's stories offers a level of stimulation that fuels his personality.

But when I asked why he dislikes being alone, he told me, "When I was alone, I had feelings that life was passing me by. To some extent, spending time alone felt like not really existing, or existing in a meaningless vacuum." For him, taking a lone walk and viewing a beautiful sunset, for example, seemed futile since no one was there to share the experience.

Some might experience a similar obstacle to feelings of futility—that of guilt about taking time for ourselves when others seem to need us almost constantly. In reality, the people in our lives often don't need us so urgently that we can't take a few minutes for ourselves. It is our own need to be needed that creates a desperate situation of constant responsibility for others that simply doesn't exist. The futility and guilt come from the lack of a foundation of self-love and acceptance. When we have that solid base, we can take responsibility for ourselves as well as others and become more effective as friends, partners, parents, or colleagues.

Over time, my client managed to learn this vital lesson of occasional solitude. "If you can envision using that time to re-energize, that's the ideal," he told me. "It has to feel like it is productive to watch a good movie alone, or get a good night's sleep alone, or contemplate the sunset alone, rather than feeling like it's a pointless nothingness or empty, lonely void."

For some, even the thought of being alone can cause great psychological trauma. Autophobia, the fear of solitude—more commonly known as Monophobia or Isolaphobia—is an extreme case and serves to indicate how serious the aversion to solitude can be. There's an unconscious aspect to the aversion to alone time. What if dark stuff comes up—all the uncomfortable thoughts, memories, beliefs, and aspects of our character we've pushed aside so that we can function in the world? I had a client who hated being alone. She was also deeply afraid of the dark. Our work included uncovering the metaphorical darkness within her so she might reclaim it and, in turn, reclaim her full self—in company or alone.

There's a distinct possibility that dark stuff will come up in your solitude. You should be thankful if it does; it's an opportunity to clear out the junk that's keeping you from being your highest self. By sifting through the murky aspects of our character, learning and claiming them as our own, we are better able to understand who we truly are. By being gentle yet honest with ourselves, by sifting through all the aspects of what makes us who we are, only then are we able to be more honest in our presence among others.

How do we get to the point of being comfortable with being alone? Go easy. Talk to others who love solitude and find out why. Take notes. Write your own. Redefine solitude for yourself.

Your Solitude Practice

One essential part of creating time alone for yourself is to recharge your batteries, making you better able to interact with others in a productive way. If you're hesitant about how to begin, or even have an outright fear of solitude, this exercise will help. Create a solitude practice project for yourself and set aside time to do it. This project should be a simple event or task. Avoid activities that include interaction with others, such as visiting social networking sites online.

Here are a few suggestions:

- Meditate
- Rent a movie
- Take a bath
- Go for a walk (no stopping to chat)
- Write in your journal

Begin treating yourself to these solitude practice projects once a week, then every other day. Work your way up to practicing solitude at least once a day.

If you feel anxious, write down what you're feeling. Make a list of your anxieties and where you think they're coming from. Be honest and clear. You can review these items later, even using the time as one of your solitude practice projects.

Blessings on the Path

God to man doth speak in solitude.
—John Stuart Blackie

Something incredible happens when you begin to spend time alone. By turning to the Self on a regular basis—listening to what your soul desires and turning down the volume on the rest of the world's perceived expectations of you—you open a channel to Source. Like a long distance phone call from home, the Great Mystery from which you came—that miraculous creative power—begins speaking clearly in your daily life.

Creation is not in the business of making things that fail. You have a unique purpose on this earth. Solitude is the only way to quiet down enough to hear what that purpose is. You'll hear it directly from Source itself.

You will begin to notice reflections of your most honest loves, your truest needs, in everything around you. Sometimes they'll literally be flung right at you. When I was living in New Mexico in my late twenties, I felt restless. I knew I was not doing what my soul wanted to do, which at that time was to pursue the acting career I'd put on hold to move out west. I spent a lot of time thinking about it, meditating on it, talking to myself about it nearly every day on my solo hour-and-fifteen-minute drive to work

> **Creation is not in the business of making things that fail. That includes you.**

from Albuquerque to Santa Fe. One morning, as usual, the newspaper was flung onto my front step. I opened it. There, in a half-page ad, was a notice for local auditions for the summer program at the American Academy of Dramatic Arts in New York City. Over the next two weeks, I got up at 6 a.m. and rehearsed monologues in my garage, preparing for a nerve-wracking 15-minute audition held at the Albuquerque Sheraton Inn.

I got into the program, packed up, and moved back to New York permanently. In my solitude, I had manifested exactly what I needed to move to the next level of my life. I call these confluences (like that newspaper showing up) Love Letters from the Universe. These Love Letters can come in all forms, not just life-altering ones. Maybe every time you meditate in your alone time you see Monarch butterflies. The next day there's a swarm of them outside your window. (Where did they come from? It's not even June!) There's no heavy significance to it; it's the Universe's way of saying, "I've got your back."

In other words, keep up the Self time. It's working for you. And when you need something else, like a life change, the universe can help you with that, too. Just check in with Self, then put it out there.

Claiming Your Self in Style

*Style is an expression of individualism mixed
with charisma. Fashion is something that
comes after style.*
—John Fairchild

For much of the time I lived alone in New York,
I worked as a senior copywriter for a multi-billion-dollar
corporation. (I won't say which one, but let's say Clive
Davis dropped by on a regular basis.) I spent weekdays
in an office, and quite a few weekend nights out on dates
with men I met through moonlighting writing gigs or
online dating sites. My wardrobe reflected this life: crisp
black trousers, white dress shirts, clingy dresses, high
heels, push-up bras. I found none of these items to be
particularly comfortable.

I yearned for flowing cotton skirts and funky
patchwork pants. Colorful leggings paired with long
Indian tunics. I had recurring fantasies about once again
owning the banana-colored classic Frye boots many of us
wore in the 1970s. But since these items were impractical
for my New York City day- and nightlife, I pushed these

desires aside.

Three years later, I left my job to start my own writing business. Now that I was working from home, there was no one to impress with my straight-out-of-*Elle*-magazine wardrobe. This thought hit me one day after my morning shower as I stood staring into my closet. "I have nothing to wear," I said to the bulging racks of neatly pressed trousers and shirts. Immediately, I grabbed handfuls of my old work clothes and stuffed them into garbage bags, which I delivered to Goodwill that very afternoon. Then I went out to a shop in "Curry Hill," Manhattan's South Asian neighborhood, and bought four gorgeous *kameezes* (Indian tunics) in the softest cotton I could find. Finally it occurred to me that because I had taken a step toward embracing life on my own terms, I could be the one to dictate my dress code. As for date nights? I figured any man who wanted to be with me would have to embrace the real me. And for the love of Joni Mitchell, the real me wanted to wear comfy clothes.

Now, I don't wish to imply that you have to quit your day job in order to reclaim your style, but you can definitely infuse your current wardrobe with items that do nothing more than please your individual sense of taste.

Should be easy to do, right? Maybe not. Many of us have spent so much time following the marching orders of the fashion and corporate worlds that we have no idea what our true style is. Here's a great way to find your style and reclaim it in the name of your Holy Self.

Eight Steps to (Re)claiming Your Own Style

Clear your mind of all you know about fashion and what image you are expected to relay with your wardrobe. This exercise is about you, no one else. If you find this difficult, just imagine for a moment that you are The Supreme Ruler of All Things and no one will question your style choices.

1. What are your favorite fabrics? Silk? Cotton? Rayon? Wool? Make a list.

2. What type of fit makes you feel good? Form-fitting? Loose and flowing? A little of both?

3. What garments seem the most "you"? (You can

answer this by taking a look at the activities that most interest you. Gardening? Sleeping? Walking? Playing sports? Reading in a comfy chair? Going out on the town?) Are you more comfortable in dresses? Skirts? Pants? Jeans? Pullovers? Button-down shirts? T-shirts?

4. If you were to combine your favorite fabric with your favorite garment, what would it look like?

5. Where might you buy or acquire such a piece?

6. Go out, get it (or make it), and put it on!

7. Congratulate yourself for taking your first step toward reclaiming your own style.

8. Repeat this exercise until your wardrobe is complete.

Addendum

Do not forget Lounge Mode. This is essential. What is Lounge Mode? It's the clothing you wear at the end of the day to put your feet up and read a book, write in your journal, listen to tunes, or indulge in a *Downton Abbey* marathon. My LM attire consists of obscenely soft yoga pants and an equally dreamy loose-fitting cotton shirt, with an occasional cotton scarf/wrap or bamboo robe, if the weather is chilly. You'll find what you like, and when you do? The end of the day won't come soon enough.

Reading, Knitting, Puzzling, Whatevering

I can elect something I love and absorb myself in it.
—Anaïs Nin

You've made the decision to carve out a chunk of alone time. Great. Now a big question looms: *What should I do?* Answer: Whatever you want. That's the beauty of spending time with your Self. These two minutes or two hours are yours to do with what *you* want. These are *your* batteries being recharged.

Your solitude practice is a wonderful opportunity to discover what makes you happy. Which projects, hobbies, interests, or obsessions you want to pursue on your time with no judgment from others. The key is to find some activity that you can turn to when in solitude that gives you unabashed pleasure. What you choose is irrelevant, so long as it rejuvenates you.

> **In your sacred space,**
> **you are in control.**
> **You are the leader,**
> **you are the lawmaker.**

One of my dearest friends is a knitting fanatic. She has probably knit, purled, and crocheted enough to clothe all the inhabitants of a small (and very cold) country. Every Friday night, we'd meet after work at the same Irish bar on Restaurant Row in New York. Each night she'd have the same shot of Crown Royal and a side of Sprite (or vice versa; I'm not sure which was the dominant beverage). I'd have the same Shiraz. Besides our attire, the only difference from week to week was whatever piece of apparel she was knitting. Yes, at the bar. My friend was so at peace with her solitary pleasure that she brought it with her everywhere she went, like a fuzzy little mohair lap dog.

My mother—queen of solitary women—is a crypotgramaholic. (There should probably be an intervention in her future, but I won't initiate it; the stacks of cryptogram books that line her bedside fill me with vicarious joy.) As for me, I'm a Bollywood addict.

And I like archery. If I have time alone, I may very well be found on my couch absorbed in a Hindi *filmi* or in the back yard slinging arrows at a big boxy target, pretending I'm an amazon. (All the while hoping I don't hit a passing UPS guy on the other side of my fence.)

A Word About Words

A big part of my solitude practice is writing in my journal. I highly recommend that everyone take up this activity. A journal is the place to record conversations with your Self-as-best-friend. You can work out existential problems, gripe about how every product you love gets discontinued right after you discover it, confess your crushes, or just log the details of the café (or park, or desk, or waiting room) where you're sitting.

No one needs to read what you write, so keeping a journal is a wonderful opportunity to explore intimate thoughts, theories, and half-baked notions with the one person who will never judge you: Your Holy Self.

You might also like to collect tokens of your life and create a series of multi-media collages. What a perfect project to celebrate your solitude. Each collage will represent in image form what is going on in your life *at that moment.* Over time, you'll have a collection of artwork, each piece of which is explicitly you. If you choose to share those pieces, others will have an opportunity to understand you better, and chances are you'll learn more about yourself as well.

Whatever you choose to do with your alone time, let it resonate with the energy that is purely you. In your sacred space, you are in control. You are the leader, you are the lawmaker. You are the only one you have to answer to.

What's My Thing?

If you're unclear about what project or hobby might speak to you, try this exercise:

1. Sit quietly and say the following, "I am looking for an activity that speaks to my truest self."
2. Take three long deep breaths in and out. (I mean, long—count to five *slowly* with each inhale and exhale.)

3. At the end of the last exhale, imagine your are pushing out all images of what "YOU" means. Push out the hard worker, the dutiful son or daughter, the taxpayer, the gym-goer, the Prius owner, the loyal supermarket shopper. All of it. Outta there.

4. As you inhale—*slowly*—you will breathe in an image. It will come to you, trust me. If it doesn't, breathe out to release more YOU stuff and try again.

5. The image you receive on your inhale will be (or will lead you to) your new project, hobby, or exercise.

Don't worry if your image seems odd. For example, if all you see is a circle with lots of colors, begin looking for things like that in your daily life. It may mean you should start painting mandalas. It could also mean you should begin baking vibrantly hued cookies or cupcakes. Your gut will know. How? You'll get that little vertigo drop in your belly that feels like you're about to kiss someone really gorgeous.

Social Networking (A Friendly Warning)

Mass communication, radio, and especially television,
have attempted, not without success, to annihilate every
possibility of solitude and reflection.
—Eugenio Montale

Your sacred alone time should not involve frooping around on Facebook, Twitter, or any other online interactive playground. The reason for this is obvious: You're not tapping into your True Self if you're checking out pics of your cousin's precocious piano-playing toddler or your friend's octopus-Carpaccio-and-martini-blind-date. These are distractions to—no, the antithesis of—your quest for Self. Social networking certainly has its place for communicating with faraway loved (and merely "like"d) ones. However, even though you may be physically alone while you check in on your pals, you are not spiritually checking in on your Self.

If the idea is to create an oasis in which to recharge your batteries for yourself and the rest of the world, then peeking into the goings on within that world (however true—or fanciful—they may be) undermines the power of Self as Guide. You're not looking inward, you're looking outward. Besides that, trolling social sites like Facebook can actually make us more lonely.

As Stephen Marche noted in his May 2012 article in *The Atlantic*:

> It's a lonely business, wandering the labyrinths of our friends' and pseudo-friends' projected identities, trying to figure out what part of ourselves we ought to project, who will listen, and what they will hear....Solitude used to be good for self-reflection and self-reinvention. But now we are left thinking about who we are all the time, without ever really thinking about who we are.

Therein lies the paradox. You're alone. What better timepass than to scan Facebook? What's the harm? You're doing Your Thing. The harm is that what you are confronted with in those scrolling gems, those well-polished nuggets of other people's "life," are the very societal expectations, roles, and status symbols that have kept you from Self all these years. (*When will I have a brilliant two-year-old? Where's my fabulous appetizer-vodka-romance? I should have those things. What's wrong with me?*) The result is further alienation from what your deepest Self wants for you. You deserve better.

The Art of Solitary Sex

Don't knock masturbation. It's sex with someone I love.
—Woody Allen

The more time you spend honoring your Holy Self, the higher the likelihood that your unique, vibrant, and essential sexuality will demand your attention at some point. Some single folks deal with sex by casually taking lovers when they wish, sort of like cleaning out the bathroom sink trap. If you're married or co-habitating, your partner is right there at your disposal most of the time. Certainly, consulting your little black book or making time for intimacy with your partner is one way to address your sexual needs. Another is to be your own lover. Developing intimate self-love is not mutually exclusive of the other ways to get your sexual needs met. In fact, it's the first step toward a more fulfilling sexual life.

If this sounds New Age-y and weird, it isn't. Think of it this way: Before you can be a good lover to anyone else, you need to be a good lover to yourself. It's that simple. What else can you bring to a sexual relationship but what you are willing to offer yourself? When someone asks you out to dinner and lets you choose the restaurant, how do you know what flavors appeal to your palate unless at one time you made the effort to figure it out on your own? Sex works the same way. The more at ease you are with your own body and your sexual needs, the better equipped you are to share sexual energy with someone else.

It's not difficult to begin developing a sense of your unique sexual identity. You can use your solitude practice to discover and encourage it in a number of ways:

- Take a warm bath. Luxuriate in the heat surrounding your body. Let the smells of your favorite bath oils fill your senses. Breathe deeply. Great bath oils to use are Lavender (stress reducer), Frankincense (anti-inflammatory; anti-depressant), Neroli (relieves depression and anxiety; rejuvenates cells) Sandalwood (promotes inner unity, calm, acceptance), Amber (meditative, sensual), or Ylang Ylang (balances male/female energy, restores confidence).

- Buy an outfit in your favorite fabric. Something loose and flowing and comfortable. (I'm a fan of linen or ultra-soft cotton.) As you wear it, be present in the way it makes you feel. Think of this outfit as a power source, filling your body with self-adoration.

- Take a dance class that focuses on sensual movements. Belly dancing is a fabulous choice for women. Bollywood/Bhangra dancing is great for men and women; it'll get your hips moving in ways you never thought were possible. If dance isn't your thing, try yoga (Vinyasa Flow, for example) or even Tai Chi and Qigong classes. Or take a rigorous spin class at your local gym. There's something deliciously primal about sweating with strangers.

- Get a massage. Having someone else caressing your body and rejuvenating it with touch is a wonderful way to meditate into your own pure sensuality. But don't zone out! Work with your massage therapist by concentrating on the area being touched. Make a point of mentally directing soothing, sensual energy to the skin and muscles being worked on.

When you're ready to move on to more concentrated sexual self-love, try this: Find a full-length mirror in your house. Get naked and stand in front of it. Even if you're not thrilled with your body right now, or if you've spent months avoiding mirrors at all costs, try not to be nervous.

You can be your own lover. How cool is that?

Now comes the fun part. As you look at your body in the mirror, don't view your body with your own eyes, but use the eyes of an imaginary lover. Someone who thinks you're a real knockout. If looking at the whole of your body is too much at once, focus on one part of your body—say, your neck. Say something nice about it. How soft it is, or how kissable it looks. Keep in mind that you are not talking as yourself; you're speaking as a lover.

Keep going. Compliment as many sections of your body as you can, even the ones you dislike. *Especially* the ones you dislike. Finally, give yourself an overall comment of admiration. What would you tell yourself if you were your own lover?

When you take time for yourself in solitude, you have a tremendous opportunity to develop a strong sense of your own sexual identity. In this way, you are better able to share your sexuality with a lover, should you choose to have one. Regardless of whether or not you have a partner, a well-developed private sexual life will help you to exude a sense of majestic self-worth.

Your Sexual Self

Create a list of ten things you like about your sexuality. No one else needs to read this list, so consider aspects of your character that even a lover might not know about you. If you need a jump-start, try answering these questions:

1. What is your first sexual memory?

2. When did you first discover your own body, sexually?

3. How do you honestly feel about sex?

4. When was your first sexual experience with another person? Was it positive? Negative? Are you indifferent? Why?

5. What was the best sexual experience you have ever had? What made it so?

6. What does "sexy" mean to you?

7. Would you say that you are a sexual person? That is, do you consider sex an important part of your life? Why or why not?

8. How satisfied are you with your current sex life?

9. What are your top three strengths as a lover?

10. What are your top three weaknesses? What do you need to turn them into strengths or eliminate them entirely?

What, Me Lonely?

You cannot be lonely if you like the person you're alone with.
—Dr. Wayne Dyer

As happy as we might be with the daily routine of single life and the ability to do whatever we want, whenever we want, there often comes a time when we may long for companionship. We may even begin to question the very nature of our solitary lives. If left unchecked, the longing and questioning can turn to brooding. That downward spiral of loneliness has an internal dialogue that might sound a little like this:

You:	Why am I alone, anyway?
Also You:	Because you want to be.
You:	Really? Did I choose this life or is it that no one wants to be around me for very long?
Also You:	Don't be silly. Here, have a donut.

You:	I don't need sugary carbs, I need an answer.
Also You:	[sighs] Well, you are a little set in your ways, but you're a very decent and loving person.
You:	You have to say that; you're me.
Also You:	Very true, oh, wise one.
You:	Seriously. Is there something wrong with me? Why does every romantic relationship I have end disastrously? Will I end up dying alone and unloved?

Et cetera, et cetera...

There are many reasons why your romantic relationships may not turn out well, so let's not dwell on that. As for dying alone? Here's a newsflash: We *all* die alone. Married people, well-loved people, people with oodles of best buddies—death is a natural journey that we all make as individuals. You don't get to bring anyone along with you. But you don't have to die unloved. In fact, spending a life alone doesn't mean remaining isolated. The truly honored Holy Self knows that it must balance the restorative properties it receives from time alone to help cultivate loving relationships with friends and family.

Loneliness is a state of mind. It usually creeps up on us when we've had a particularly bad day (or week, or month) and are feeling defeated. Here's something that will make you feel better: Loneliness may be a sign that you've done an excellent job of honoring your Holy Self. Your soul's batteries are now well charged and it's time to go out and socialize.

> **Spending a life alone doesn't mean remaining isolated.**

What if no one you know is around or free to play with you? Go out anyway. Here are a few things you can do to combat loneliness:

- Volunteer...*anywhere*. Soup kitchen, YMCA, after-school programs for kids, etc.
- Go to a poetry reading or book signing at your local bookstore.
- Go to the gym and work your loneliness off in a

group class.

- Take a course in something you've always wanted to learn at your community center.

Here's what *not* to do if you're feeling lonely:

- Think about how lonely you are.
- Ask yourself why no one wants to be with you.
- Eat a pint of Ben and Jerry's Mud Pie ice cream while staring blankly at the refrigerator door magnets.

> **Turn negative loneliness into positive aloneness.**

After about three or four years in a row of living alone, I began to experience a deep longing for companionship, and the inevitable questioning that accompanied not finding True Love. I paced around my house talking out loud to myself about how it might be possible to be pushing forty and still single. I had no terrible habits (except, perhaps, talking out loud to myself). I was neat, clean, funny, intelligent, and a good listener. I could make a mean salad. I had

decent if eclectic taste in music, literature, art, cinema...
So what was going wrong? Why was I single? Why didn't
I have loads of friends to keep me afloat (instead of a
small handful, most of whom lived in different states)?
As I paced and talked, I found myself descending into a
depression. It was a depression based on the fear that
there was something fundamentally wrong with me and
I would remain on the fringes of society forevermore.

I had to stop the spiral. How? By turning off the
stream of negative ideas in my head and allowing the
positive facts of my life seep in. The distinction is an
important one, so let me say it again: I stopped the
negative *ideas* and let the positive *facts* take over.

Loneliness is a state of mind. Negative ideas
encircle that state, thoughts of being abandoned or of
not being worthy of human interaction. By turning those
thoughts off—simply not letting them have airtime in
our minds—we leave room to cultivate positive facts
about our life alone. For example, instead of, "What if
secretly no one really likes me?" think: "In my life alone,
I have time and peace of mind to accomplish my goals."
In essence, we can turn negative loneliness into positive
aloneness.

Stopping the Downward Spiral of Negativity

Stopping the flow of negative thoughts may seem easier said than done. In reality, what you are doing is retraining your mind to think a certain way. Scientists have proven that certain thought patterns create a neural pathway in your brain, much like a well-worn hiking trail in the woods. It's your job to step off the negative path and blaze a new one with positivity. This is how hypnotherapy works, and its tools can be used by anyone.

The next time you feel lonely to the point of questioning your life of solitude, isolate the first negative thought that comes to you. Write it down. Now consider a positive aspect of your life alone. Perhaps it's the clarity of mind that comes from living a home life without interruption from others. Or it's the joy of knowing each day can unfold as you desire, with no one to question your decisions. Write the positive fact of your life down as well.

You may even wish to put a blank sheet of paper on the refrigerator and add your positive facts as they come to you. Refer to it often for a quick pep talk, especially when you feel the negative thoughts creeping in.

Family and Friends

I don't need a man to rectify my existence. The most profound relationship we'll ever have is the one with ourselves.
—Shirley MacLaine

When you live alone, the importance of having a solid base of loving family and friends cannot be overstated. These people are our support system and keep us from spending too much time in our own heads. As vital as time alone is to recharge our soul's batteries, we also need to reconnect with the world, lend ourselves to others, and learn from them. This ebb and flow of communication fuels us and reminds us that even though we live alone, we are not entirely on our own. Rather, all of us are interconnected—with our loved ones as well as with everything in the universe. But let's start a little smaller than the entire universe.

Family

Depending on the type of family you come from, you may find that your single life is either accepted wholeheartedly or viewed with a tinge of pity. If you're lucky, holidays at home are not peppered with hints about finding that special someone to bring home *next* year. Playing with your siblings' children doesn't paint your family's faces with shades of expectation that you, too, might add a leaf to the family tree with one of your own. If you're lucky, your life as a single person is met with joy and encouragement, and the knowledge that you're out there living life fully.

If you're lucky.

If not, here are a few tips for helping your family along when you're being pushed to explain your life of solitude or are outright attacked for it:

1. Take a deep breath and remember that your family loves you. If they didn't, they wouldn't bother worrying about you.

2. Smile. (A real smile, not that fake, I'm-tolerating-you smile.)

3. Tell whomever it is you're talking to that you are happy. You are peaceful in the choice you've made to live alone. You're not opposed to finding True Love (unless you are, in which case,

Celebrating Solitude

skip this part), but right now you're living your life as best you can. Yes, life can get a little lonesome at times, but that's where the love of good friends and family (like you, dear mother/father/sister/brother/aunt/etc.)   comes in. Thank the person for his concern. Give him a hug.

4.   Suggest a distraction like tag football or a slice of pie. Anything. Change the subject.

Friends

I've found that friends are often more accepting than family of the solitary lifestyle. In fact, many prefer having friends they can rely on any time of the day or night for quick pep talks or a shoulder to cry on (or a phone to text to). But, of course, true friends love you regardless of your relationship status.

After the end of a long-term relationship, I began a five-year stint of solitude. I made good friends with my new apartment neighbors, Bruce and Bob, who lived just one floor below. They regularly held impromptu late-night cocktail parties, which I often attended in my pajamas. When my cat Winnie died, they were there for me when I discovered her under my bed at half-past midnight and was too distraught to remove her myself. Before my first trip to India, Bob tended to me during the sudden illness brought on by four inoculations playing doubles tennis in my bloodstream. My life of solitude was greatly enriched by their love, respect, and Bruce's famous cheesy garlic bread. When I got married five years later, they were there to cheer me with a glass of champagne and whoops of joy.

Of course, Bruce and Bob are by no means the only beloved friends I have, but when I was alone—and sometimes lonely—they were nearly always there to cheer me.

You know who your friends are. Take a moment to be thankful for them. Love them. Cherish them. Use their strength when you need it. Recharge your own soul in your solitary times so that you can give back to them when they need you. This is what any friendship is about, but for those of us who live alone, friendships remind us that as we dance along our path, our friends are right there beside us, dancing on their own. You can reach hands across and touch now and again, never breaking your own individual strides. What a blessing!

Card Them

Make a list of your dearest friends and family members. Send each of them a card that expresses your love and thanks. No, it's not corny. Trust me, they'll love it. And you'll be putting good energy out into the universe. Everyone wins.

Dating and Relationships

Dating is about finding out who you are and who others are. If you show up in a masquerade outfit, neither is going to happen.
—Henry Cloud

When I was single, I met many of the men I dated through online dating services. It required an awful lot of administrative work to maintain the five—yes, five—dating sites I subscribed to. I was plucky about the whole thing, determined to find my soul mate. I remained undeterred even when one man's profile read, "Must love goats." (I'm not kidding.)

After a while, however, I became frustrated by constant commiserating with girlfriends who were also dating about how there simply *must* be someone out there for us. Underneath our conversations was the paralyzing fear: What if there *isn't?*

Yes, I wondered. *What then?*

Then? It's a life alone...just like the one I'd been living and enjoying. Almost every single person on the hunt for a partner has heard the aggravating advice:

"When you stop looking, you'll find someone." Perhaps you've even taken this advice. It works for a while, abstaining from romantic dealings for a week or two only to wake up one Saturday morning at 2 a.m. on the couch in a pool of drool with the DVD menu of *Nurse Betty* looping on your TV. You've just spent another Friday night alone. Not so satisfying after all.

The fear kicks in that this is how you'll die. It'll be death by romantic comedy or by choking on a popcorn kernel. No one will find your body for weeks. And, oh! The stigma of a 40-something single guy or gal! If you're not Oprah or George Clooney, you're convinced, it ain't workin'. How hard you'll have to work to prove yourself a valid member of society, a success...and *not jaded.*

Give it up.

**Solitude is your best friend.
When you come home from a date,
tell it how things went.
If things don't work out, your solitude
will be there for you.**

If you live alone and date, needless to say you don't need tips on finding time for solitude. What you do need is to begin to honor that solitude. Take a small nugget of your beloved aloneness with you on your dates. Doing this will help you keep your expectations at a reasonable level.

If you're in a new relationship, the advice is the same. There will be a time (if there isn't already) when you've fallen madly in love and can't imagine spending a moment apart, not even for a bathroom break. Remember and love your solitude then, too.

One of the greatest pleasures is coming home after a great date and luxuriating in all the memories of your time together. Your solitude is your best friend. Tell it out loud how your date gave you a surprise kiss right on Main Street. Or how he smelled. Or how right it felt sitting so close to her at the restaurant.

And if things don't work out? Whether the relationship tanks after the first or the twenty-first date, your solitude will buoy you up. You're not retreating to a lonely life, you're continuing the eternal love affair you have with your Self.

Here's a secret: Even if you marry, that love

affair continues, so nurture it now.

Remember that you cannot make anyone love you. No amount of primping, push-upping, pumping weights, or waxing is going to create love where it cannot be. This fact is a gift from the universe. Take it. Why?

The amount of primping you do for a date is directly proportional to how badly you'll feel if things don't work out.

Take it easy and be yourself.

Because of one very vital thing: If you're with the wrong person, you are therefore unavailable for the right one.

Do not compromise. Ever. Do not undervalue your Holy Self. Develop a loving relationship with yourself. Use your time alone to replenish, refresh, and recharge your soul's batteries. Then get out there and dazzle the world with *you*.

The Social Club

Dating is a wonderful opportunity to meet other people. Think of it as a social club. When you've made plans for the next date, try this:

- Wear an outfit created with the "Claim Your Self in Style" chapter.

- Meditate before the date.

- Plan an after-hours date with yourself. Treat yourself to a movie rental. Have a cup of expensive tea. Write in your journal. Choose something you'll look forward to.

The Bed

When I'm alone, I can sleep crossways in bed without an argument.
—Zsa Zsa Gabor

Ah, bed. That most underappreciated slab of furniture. It lies in your bedroom, spending sixteen hours of the day unused, perhaps even unmade, waiting patiently for your weary return...

What is a bed for? Many will say that a bed has only two functions: sleep and sex. While that is certainly true, for the single woman or man, bed can be so much more! It can be your sanctuary, your entertainment hub, your command center.

I love bed. If I could spend my life between bed, the outdoors, and a few nice cafés I like to hang out in, I'd do it in a flash. I even love the phrase, *took to bed.* As in, *Miss Eleanor was overcome and took to her bed.* The idea of retreating to a pillowy wonderland designed solely for your comfort seems pretty darned delicious to me.

The Sanctuary

We often overlook the importance of physical comfort. We buy shoes that look fabulous but wearing them is akin to medieval torture. Upgrading your bedding is an easy way to infuse comfort into your life. And it's not necessarily expensive to outfit your bed for maximum comfiness.

On a basic level, one of the bed's primary functions is to provide comfort. Therefore, as a first step, it's essential to set your bed up for sumptuous relaxation. With my own bed, I try to achieve a quality that I call "numminess." Nummy is that safe and snuggly feeling you get when you pull the covers tight around you and recline against your pillow. It's a bliss right up there with really good sex. That's why it's vital that you begin with the preparation of your bed. Even if sleep and sex *are* the only functions it ever has, you'll have given yourself a great gift.

We can also think of our bed as a decompression chamber. A natural form of meditation is to simply lie in bed and stare at the ceiling (or the wall, or out the window) to let our minds clear a bit. The stresses of our everyday lives—careers, relationships, and family—necessitate a break of this nature. Bed is there for you.

The Entertainment Hub

For many, the idea of bed as a location for entertaining oneself is a no-no. But when you live alone, the bed can be a terrific place to set up camp for prime enjoyment.

Unlike many, I do not have a problem with having a television in the bedroom. I think of it like alcohol: a little can be a lovely thing. Healthy, even. Abusing the privilege, however, is not advised.

There's something deliciously naughty about crawling into bed and cozying up to a good old movie. A television in the bedroom is also a fine companion for occasional loneliness jags. I know from experience that there are immense healing properties to the combination of a comfy bed and a Mel Brooks film festival.

**Invest in a good lap desk
or breakfast tray with legs.**

For those opposed to having portals of electronic media in the bedroom, your bed is also a great place to get reading done. Dust off your library card and get caught up on your favorite mysteries, the classics you never got around to, or work your way through the *New York Times* Best Seller list. The important thing is to use your solitary bed-time to pamper yourself.

Writing in bed is another pleasure. I've logged many a journal entry nestled between my Egyptian cotton sheets. I keep a blank notebook and pen by the bed as well, in case the muse decides to drop by at four-thirty in the morning. It happens. Let me tell you, it's immensely frustrating to think you've committed a great thought to memory, but when the sun rises, all you can remember is a fuzzy something about red kites and salamanders.

The Command Center

Many of us have dragged the laptop into bed to fire off a few emails or putter around on Facebook, but get this: I once dated a man who hooked his computer up to the huge-screened television in his bedroom, using it as a monitor instead of his laptop's paltry 15-inch screen. Talk about using your bed as a command center!

In a similar vein, my mother has made an art of her solitary bed-time. Not only is her queen-sized sanctuary bedecked in the fluffiest comforters, pillows, and sheets, she has everything she could possibly want at arm's reach, from *New York Times* crossword puzzles to candied peanuts. If that weren't enough, for her morning ritual she has—I kid you not—a small coffee pot set up so that all she needs to do is roll over for her first cup of joe. Hey, if you're going to do it, do it right.

Pimping Your Ride: Setting Your Bed Up for Comfort

The Mattress

The first step to creating a bed sanctuary is to buy the right mattress. In order to do this, you must shop at a brick-and-mortar bed store. Online shopping will not suffice for something as crucial as bed-buying. Feeling is believing.

Upon arriving at the store, you'll need to tell the salesperson who will inevitably descend upon you like a fruit fly on an overripe banana that you're just looking and you'll let him know when you need help. Then do yourself a favor and forget he's there (until you actually need him). Lie down on many different models for several minutes. Sit up, too, since you might be reading, writing, or watching a movie in bed. Does your body instantly relax? How is the support under your spine?

Let's say you've found your dream mattress, but you're fretting about the price tag. If you're concerned, think of this: Unlike that $2,000 monstrosity of a step machine you bought, your bed is something you'll use every day. Mattresses need to be replaced every seven years or so. So, if you splurge on a $1,500 queen-sized mattress, you're spending under sixty cents a day on your health and comfort. As smart investments go, that's brilliant.

The Bedding

Here's where you get really creative. The right bedding makes the bed and defines the level of comfort you're going to experience. Here again, indulge yourself.

Sheets: When buying sheets, don't even look at anything under 300 count. My preference is 100% Egyptian cotton, but not sateen. (They feel slippery to me.) You don't have to go high-end. Some of the best sheets I've slept on were old white cotton sheets at a mid-range hotel in Negril, Jamaica. I asked the owner what brand they were, and she shrugged: "Plain cotton." So, there you go. The key is washing them a lot so they get ultra-soft, thereby developing a high numminess factor.

Comforter: A good all-seasons down comforter will set you back about $100. If you buy quality, you get quality. That means you can still use your fluffy comforter in the oppressive heat of summer. Go for box stitching to maintain loft and avoid hot and cold spots. Buy a duvet cover for your comforter that matches your sheets' texture and quality.

Pillows: I like to mix things up here. I have a firmish, memory foam, standard-sized pillow that I use to support my head. I also have a king-sized pillow that I use as my BFP (Boyfriend Pillow), thusly named not only for the way it's held (placed perpendicularly to the head pillow and clutched tight during sleep), but because a lover with a bad back enlightened me to its therapeutic benefits; the BFP (or GFP, as you prefer) is ideal for wedging between your knees as you sleep.

The good news is that most of your bedding items can be purchased online at discount stores. I managed to put together my whole luxurious bedding extravaganza for under $300.

So. You've made your bed, now... Well, you know the rest.

Making Time

We visit others as a matter of social obligation.
How long has it been since we have visited with ourselves?
—Morris Adler

There is one very important aspect of creating a solitude practice: Making time to do it. For those living alone, solitary time is a given, but what about those who live with a partner and/or have families? It may seem an impossible feat—not to mention a frivolous luxury—to take time away from our responsibilities to those we live with (and the shopping, cooking, cleaning, and fresh laundry they require). It is possible, however.

If you share your home with one other person, you may feel that it would be eccentric, rude, or selfish to request a chunk of time for yourself. Don't. As we've discussed before and will again, solitary time is helpful for everyone, so you may try offering that you *and* your partner reserve a bit of time to recharge your batteries. If you do your solitude practice simultaneously, both of you will benefit without cutting into the flow of your day-to-day life together. If your partner is not interested, explain the concept of recharging your batteries, and how it's a necessity for you in order to be the best partner you can be. Make

> **Alone time is for your soul what going to the gym is for your body.**

sure that the message gets through in a loving manner, not a defensive one. You don't want your partner to feel unworthy of your time or blamed for your need to be alone a while. Explain that solitary time is for you, but ultimately everyone around you will feel its positive effects. It's hard to fault that logic.

If you have a family of three or more, you may feel like there's no possible way you could afford such time, never mind ask for it. The first step is to take a look at your existing schedule. Are there any moments in the day that can be parceled out for just you?

One of my dearest friends, and an expert at honoring her Holy Self, takes her solitary time very early in the morning before her husband and two children are awake. She makes a pot of coffee and sits at the kitchen table alone writing and staring out at the sunrise from her kitchen window. She tells me that without this little bit of quiet alone time, she'd be a wreck for the rest of the day.

Perhaps dawn works for you. It doesn't work well for me as the mother of a young child who isn't fond of lounging abed in the morning; I cherish my early morning sleep hours. Instead, I take my solitary time at night, after everyone has gone to bed. Or in the day, after my work is done, and while my son is at school. If you don't have help during the day, try these options:

- Ask your partner to watch the child(ren) while you enjoy your solitude practice.
- If you have older children, explain to them that you're taking some time for yourself so that you'll be a happier parent. (See "The Closed Door" chapter.)
- Consider scheduling your solitude practice for after the kids have gone to sleep.

So, how much time can you realistically take? Since many of us with family lives have busy and erratic schedules, you can't expect to claim an hour for yourself every day. Even five minutes of concentrated solitary time can do wonders. The important thing is that you take whatever time you can once a day, set the intention, and claim it as your own. Alone time is to the soul what going to the gym is to the body. It may seem difficult to make a regular commitment, but the benefits are tremendous. And solitude has one advantage over going to the gym (besides being significantly less expensive). While the gym gets your body and mind in better shape, the benefits stop there. A regular solitude practice benefits you *and* your family. Pretty good deal, wouldn't you agree?

The Closed Door

When one door is closed, don't you know, another is open.
—Bob Marley

When I began working on this book, I often heard my then infant son downstairs crying in the arms of the part-time nanny I hired so I could write. You want guilt? There's a heaping helping of it. I kept thinking: *I should be with him. He's a baby, for goodness' sake. What kind of mother am I?* Every morning, I heard *selfish, selfish, selfish* in the churning motor of my breast pump. But I knew there was only one way to gather up regenerative time and space for myself while working at home: I had to close the door.

As partners and/or parents, we need to recharge more than most. We spend so much time tending to the needs of others that it is not a luxury but a necessity for us to take a few minutes a day for ourselves. If we don't, we're no good to anyone. Maybe not right away, but mark my words, going without self-time for too long will result in a very unpleasant and oftentimes irrational meltdown.

Choose a sacred space for yourself whether it's in your bedroom, home office, or study. Preferably somewhere with a door. The closed door is a symbol. It says to your partner/family, "Do not disturb me unless there is an emergency." Emergency means the house is on fire. Or someone's been electrocuted. Or impaled himself on a dinner fork. In order to ensure you have your much-needed

> **Going without self-time for too long will result in a very unpleasant meltdown.**

solitude, you must enforce the symbol of the closed door.

Getting your family to respect the closed door may be tricky at first. Every lost tape dispenser or broken toy may seem like an emergency worthy of disturbing you. Not to mention that kids might find it suspect; they often associate spending time alone with something that happens when they paint the cat with mustard. Don't give up, though. Keep staking out your time and space. Remind everyone that you'll be back in a few minutes. If your kids have trouble honoring your time alone, work together to create a "Daddy (or Mommy) Time:

Shhhhhh!" sign that you can hang on the door. When you discuss your time alone with your family, do so with a positive attitude. It will help them understand that while it may seem like you're abandoning the family, in reality, you're giving them a gift: A few minutes to yourself a day will help you be a better partner/parent.

Introducing the Closed Door

Introducing the closed door to your partner and family is not as difficult as it might seem. Here is a three-step process that should help.

Communicate Clearly

Gather your family in front of the door of the room in which you intend to have your solitary time. Tell them, "This is the door. When it's closed, I'm not to be disturbed unless there's an emergency." Define emergency: Someone is hurt or in serious danger. Explain to them what you are going to be doing in general terms. You may wish to keep it simple and say you are meditating or taking time for yourself. Go over the rules with an upbeat attitude, so that it's clear you are doing a helpful thing for yourself and for them.

Trial Run

The first time you utilize the closed door, take only a few minutes for your solitude practice. No more than ten. Don't expect much and don't plan to get too involved with your journal-writing, meditating, or whatever your rejuvenating event might be.

If you are interrupted, keep the door shut and communicate through it. Possible scenarios:

[*knock, knock*]

Husband:	Sorry, I know you're busy, but where's that apple-slicing thing?
You:	That's not an emergency, right, my dearest love? I'll be out soon.

Or:

[*knock, knock*]

Child:	Max won't give me the iPad. I said please.
You:	That's not a real emergency, sweetheart. Daddy will be out in six minutes.

Give everyone a grace period of a few days to get used to honoring your request for privacy during your solitude. After that period is over, if you are still interrupted, begin to be more forceful—yet always loving—in your responses to non-emergent disturbances.

Scheduling

Begin to take time for yourself every other day. After a week or so, increase to once a day. In this way, your family will get used to your time alone. If possible, choose the same time of day in order to enforce your solitude's regularity.

Above all, stick with it. Closing a door on your loved ones may seem hard or even pointless at first, but not only is it worth it, it's vital for you and for them.

The Guardians at the Gate:
Aversion, Jealousy, and Resentment

Happiness and contentment...can be experienced only by the individual and not by a State, which...continually threatens to paralyze and suppress the individual.
—C.G. Jung

As you begin your solitude practice, you may encounter some resistance from your partner. That resistance could be coming from two places. First, there's an aversion to one's mate going off to do his own thing. Second, your partner may feel jealous. Behind the aversion and jealousy is the possible translation of "I need some time alone" to "I need to be away from *you.*" Initially, your partner may feel rejected and wonder what he did wrong to send you away.

Keep in mind that both types of resistance come from ingrained behavior that was originally designed to protect us in the big scary world out there—a Darwinian concept based on safety in numbers. Stay close to the group and you'll be safe from predators. Go it alone and you might get killed. Sticking with the crowd—and being accepted by it—ensured our ongoing existence.

However, over the last century, mental health professionals have learned that blindly following the masses often leads to misery in later life. We become psychological automatons, never tapping into and honoring our individual selves. In some cases, not even knowing we have an individual self beyond the I-being which is separate from the You-being. We have a conscious knowledge that we are as unique as a snowflake; it's a common theme we learn as early as grade school. Yet as we face our mortality, we realize that we have done nothing to even remotely celebrate that uniqueness. We don't need to create monuments or cure diseases. But we do need to take Deepak Chopra's advice to not think out of the box, but get rid of the box entirely.

In his book, *The Undiscovered Self*, depth psychologist Carl Jung refers to this necessary breaking from the crowd as "individuation." By taking time for

> **You are establishing a self that will be the bedrock of all you do and all you are for the rest of your life.**

yourself, you are individuating. You are establishing a self that will be the bedrock of all you do and all you are for the rest of your life.

This brings up another, unconscious form of jealousy your partner may be experiencing: Resentment over the loving attention you're giving yourself. Your self-celebration sets off a feeling of loss as she looks at the lack of self-celebration in her own life. Believe it or not, this feeling is a tremendous gift. Darkness merely points out a lack of light. You can actually help your loved one turn on her inner light and overcome feelings of discomfort about you taking time for yourself. The easiest way to do that is to be honest. Explain to your partner why taking up a solitude practice is so important. Give a gentle reminder that this is not an act of isolation, but rather a refreshing of your soul's energies so that you can be more revitalized for yourself and everyone around you.

Above all, remind your partner that a solitude practice is not exclusive! Suggest that he might benefit from time some alone time as well. Share the wealth.

Share the Wealth

Let there be space in your togetherness.
—Khalil Gibran

This chapter is a quick reference guide for ways everyone in your household—individual partners and children alike—can incorporate alone time into their lives as a regular practice.

Make it a family affair. Just like together time at the dinner table or on a trip to the beach, take solitude time simultaneously as a family. (If there are young children in your family, be sure they are in a safe environment during their solitude practice.)

Make a collage. Invite kids to find pictures of things they like to do alone and make a collage that they can hang in their rooms or wherever they take their solitude break.

Chart it. Children might enjoy making a chart of rotating alone time activities. Post it in the kitchen. For example, Mondays are for reading a book; Tuesdays are for painting; Wednesday is "Write a Story" day; etc. Each child can make his own chart.

Talk about it. Have a family discussion or circle time about the experiences of your respective solitude sessions. Talk about the ways this practice might help you in your daily life. Get specific.

Honor resistance. Keep in mind that not everyone in the family may be interested in spending time alone. If your partner or child resists, don't force it. You can encourage a reluctant child to take part in alone time by suggesting how fun it will be to get together afterwards to share thoughts and feelings, or even to offer up what he or she has done during the time alone—a kind of show-and-tell at home.

If your child still does not wish to participate, consider staggering alone times with your partner so that your child doesn't feel left out.

Encourage a non-participating child to make a chart of alone time projects anyway. Do those projects with the child while everyone else is taking time for themselves.

If you choose to reconvene as a family after alone time, be sure the non-participating child takes part in the discussion or show-and-tell. By keeping her in the loop, over time she may wish to try alone time as well.

The ideal situation is a once-a-day event where all members of the family simultaneously retire to their respective sacred spaces, recharge, then reunite happier, healthier, and more whole. If this happens for your family, wonderful! If not, honor each family member's needs—including your own.

Solitude and Spirituality

Sacred Space

Your sacred space is where you can find yourself again and again.
—Joseph Campbell

A key part of your solitude practice is finding a peaceful place that makes you comfortable and inspires the development of your Holy Self. We'll call this your Sacred Space. In the best of all possible worlds, you'll return to this Sacred Space every time you take your alone time. Even if you only get to it once a week or so, it's very important to create a Sacred Space as a symbol of your quest to discover and nurture your Holy Self.

Don't feel you have to devote an entire room to your solitude practice, but that would certainly be the ideal. There are many options for you to choose from. Find whatever resonates with you. Below are a few ideas to get your imagination going. Choose what works best with your lifestyle.

A room of your own. If you have a spare bedroom in your house, claim it as your Sacred Space. Even a large closet works well. Or an unused pantry. Take a look around your home to see if there are any spaces that could be consolidated and cleared out to allow room for you.

> **It is vital to create a Sacred Space so that you are reminded of your quest to discover and nurture your Holy Self.**

Head outdoors. If you live in an area with nice weather and have a shed or similar structure outside, you can turn it into your Sacred Space. If your only time to practice is a lunch break at work, find a park. Claim a specific area that you will return to each session.

Go to your corner. If you live alone, an ideal spot for your Sacred Space is a corner of your bedroom or living room. (If you co-habitate, make sure your partner doesn't mind.) The bedroom is preferred, since you'll have a door to close for maximum privacy. You may wish to set up a tri-panel screen to section off your area. They are relatively inexpensive, and you can even decorate it to suit your personal tastes.

Shelf it. If you're really low on space, a simple shelf or a dedicated accent table will do the trick. You'll fill this space—or any other—with your Power Items, which we'll discuss in the next chapter. Again, try to section off this area with a screen or place it in an area with low traffic.

A former partner and I used to share a studio apartment near the United Nations. Apartments in New York are notoriously small; you can imagine the kind of cramped quarters a studio would offer. We both practiced meditation, so finding our Sacred Space was quite a challenge. There happened to be a loft-type ledge in the main living area that was probably intended for storage. We found that if we stood on the couch, we could climb up into it rather easily. And to our surprise, the ledge was just wide enough for a *zabuton* (square meditation cushion) as well as an incense holder, a candle, and a few other meditation accoutrements we liked to have around. What luck! You can see that almost any home arrangement will accommodate your Sacred Space; you just have to get creative.

Finding Your Power Items

I have a lot of objects in my space—little things,
reminders, memories.
—Marc Newson

Once you've established your Sacred Space, you'll need to add items, objects, totems that make it sacred. What might those items be and where can you find them? You and you alone get to decide what belongs in your Sacred Space. That's the whole idea. When you hunt for power items, use only your own desires as a guide. Anything—*anything*—can be placed in your space so long as it speaks to you directly and resonates with the power of your highest self.

There's only one rule: Forget what you think belongs in a Sacred Space. Let your gut choose your items. As Walt Whitman wrote, "dismiss whatever insults your own soul." If you're not a fan of candles or incense, leave them out. Conversely, if some object speaks to you even though it might seem like an odd thing to have in a "sacred" space, add it anyway. No one is watching or judging you; put that lucky pink bunny rabbit keychain in your space. The more you adhere to your purest instincts, the more powerful your space will be.

Still stuck? Take a suggestion from the ancients. For thousands of years sacred spaces have included items that represent the Four Directions/Elements: East/Air; South/Fire; West/Water; North/Earth. Or you might create a theme for your Sacred Space that will support areas of your life you'd like to enhance such as Positivity, Abundance, Health, or Loving Kindness. All that matters is that you select individual items that resonate with you.

Here are a few ideas:

- Rocks
- Feathers
- A small sculpture of your favorite animal
- Gemstones
- Water
- Meaningful jewelry
- Photographs of loved ones or teachers
- Driftwood
- Pottery
- Candles

- Your journal

- Sea glass

- Drums/rattles

- Offering bowl (to fill with whatever pleases you and changed as desired)

- Incense

- Fabric

- Fresh or dried flowers

**You alone get to decide what belongs in your Sacred Space.
That's the whole idea.**

Once you've collected a fair amount of items, you can "charge" them by saying a few words of welcome and asking that they assist you in creating and maintaining your Holy Self. Burning white sage and wafting the smoke over the items is a powerful way to cleanse them and change their energy for your purpose. Whatever you do to welcome your items will be a powerful ritual that transforms your own attitude toward your Sacred Space by creating a bridge between the mundane and the Divine.

Power Item Hunt

If you're not sure where to begin finding power items, try this exercise.

Go outside. Take a deep breath and set your intention to find a Power Item. Begin walking around the area where you live. Keep an eye out for one object that seems to leap out at you, "glow," or even just give you a sense of knowing in your belly. Pick it up and hold it to you to make sure the powerful feelings remain. If so, bring it back to your Sacred Space. Do this as often as needed.

Meditation

Meditation is the soul's perspective glass.
—Owen Feltham

Many, many books have been written about meditation. I've read a good number of them, from Zen Buddhist practices to Kundalini yoga. I began meditating at the age of twenty-one. My regular practice was shoddy at times, to say the least. I often felt I couldn't sacrifice an hour of my day to sit and do nothing. *Think* nothing. After all, that's the principle of most meditational practices: Strive to have no thoughts. When I meditated, a thought arose and my conscious mind said, "That's bad. I'm supposed to have *no* thoughts. I have to stretch out the space *between* thoughts. I suck at this!" And then I had to start over.

It wasn't until I began studying Dzogchen, a Tibetan Buddhist teaching, that I realized meditation had a much broader definition. In Dzogchen, the idea is to clear the mind of "dual" thoughts. That is, judgments about what is good and bad, worthy and useless, etc.

Thoughts will arise—we're conscious beings—but attach no significance to them. As Dzogchen master Chögyal Namkhai Norbu says, we should observe thoughts as a mirror reflects images. They are just there. Then they move away. The mirror does not judge the images as right or wrong, good or bad. Other techniques suggest

> **Meditation is *your* time.**
> **No one is watching or judging you.**
> **Go ahead and enjoy yourself.**

you consider thoughts as you would clouds in the sky. We'd never try to hold onto a cloud. That's silly. Not to mention impossible. We let it float across the sky, without judgment. There's no, "Man, that cloud is stupid." I don't know about you, but I found this lesson to be a great relief. Now I could sit, be peaceful, and let my random thoughts float across the sky of my mind, free from the burden of categorizing or valuing them.

It's with this premise that you can begin your meditation practice. We've established that our regenerative energy needs solitude to thrive. Sometimes our minds become so cluttered with the stresses of our life that no matter what activities we use to unwind and reconnect with Self—reading, writing, seeing a film, taking a bath—the stress never lets us fully recharge. In that way, meditation is a helpful tool.

Now, before you dismiss the idea of meditating as being too lofty for you, give it a try. Even if you've tried before and hated it, try again. You may find this helpful: Your meditation sessions don't have to be an hour long. Or even half an hour. You can start with five minutes. Or two. A full 120 seconds devoted to clearing your mind and relaxing your body will do wonders for twenty-four hours straight of daily stress. Besides, even the busiest parent or CEO has the ability let go of the daily grind for 120 seconds.

Micro-meditation in Ten Steps

This meditation practice is designed to be done quickly, but keep in mind that it must be done fully, with awareness and positive intention. You're devoting a minimum of two minutes to your own health. Take it seriously. Ideally you'll want to practice this meditation every day.

1. Go to your Sacred Space. Light your candles and/or incense. Whatever your instincts tell you will help you relax.

2. Set your clock for the length of time you wish to meditate. Start with two minutes if you wish. Or go for five minutes to start. (Eventually you won't need to set a clock; you'll know instinctively when it's time to stop.)

3. Sit comfortably on a pillow or chair with a straight back. Don't lie down or you might fall asleep.

4. Close your eyes or keep your eyes focused on an object (candle flame, god or goddess statue, inspirational painting, photo of a beloved teacher).

5. Take a slow, *deep* breath in through your nose and out through your mouth.

6. Continue deep breathing in this manner until your body naturally begins to breathe calmly on its own.

7. Now turn your attention to your body. Relax all the muscles you can and still remain upright.

Imagine your body dissolving into the air around you.

8. As thoughts arise, do not judge them or pay attention to them. Let them drift by, like clouds in the sky.

9. As your time ends, take another cleansing breath—in through the nose and out through the mouth.

10. You may wish to end with an affirmation or set an intention for your day. Say thank you to yourself, your higher power, The Universe— whatever you feel is a good way to honor your practice.

Gut Check

How are you doing?

By this point, you probably appreciate the pragmatic value of creating a regular solitude practice. But you may also still have some resistance. If you are feeling resistance, I invite you to ask yourself why.

Get a piece of paper and write down all the reasons until you have no more to say. Go through your list. For each reason ask yourself: *How is this belief serving me?*

If a thought or feeling is not serving you, get rid of it. Be ruthless. This is about your well-being. Bring your mind back to the benefits of beginning a solitude practice.

By the end of the exercise, chances are you will discover that the choice to avoid solitude is not as valuable as taking even 120 seconds a day to honor your Self.

Dancing in the Temple of the Holy Self

Grace is within you. If it were external, it would be useless.
—Ramana Maharshi

There's even more relevance to self-celebration than simply recharging your soul's batteries so that you can radiate your unique power to loved ones as well as yourself. There's a great majesty in the very act of taking quiet moments for yourself. Every time you to turn inward without fear and honor the time you spend with the life-long companion that you are, you connect directly to Source. It's your big THANK YOU to Creation. That's because by being fully You, you are living up to what Creation had in mind.

**Every time you honor your Self,
you are saying
Thank you to Creation.**

Each being in existence is here to live its own path, at its own pace, learning the lessons set before it in this lifetime. Stop rushing around. Stop comparing yourself to others. Can you imagine a rose spending its brief life trying to be a sunflower? What a waste! A tree has no responsibility but to live its treeness. It has only to be the tree-est tree it can be. A rock's responsibility is its pure rockness, being the rockest rock it can be. Celebrate your –ness. Be the youest you. If spend your life struggling to be other than what you are right now—yes, right this very moment—you are doing a disservice to yourself and to the Great Mystery that created you. Be the best You you can be. No one wants anything less or more of you. And the best part is, only you know what that best You is.

This is the core of solitude practice. Getting to learn all the colors and textures and loves and aversions and darknesses and radiance that make you unique. And for the love of figgy pudding, have *fun* with the process! Dance in your temple. When you do, Creation will feel you shaking the ground with your own miraculous feet. There's no better way to give thanks for your life than that.

Over time, you'll find that your Holy Self is with you wherever you go. Imagine: No more frustrating waits in line at the grocery store. You have *you* to play with. As you stand behind the man with three dozen frozen dinners inching their way toward the checkout scanner like Arctic icebergs, think about your next solitude session and what projects you might work on. If your soul's battery is sufficiently juiced, you can devote the time in line to your loved ones or colleagues and their needs. If none of that appeals, fantasize about what you'd name a planet if you discovered one. Or solve the world hunger crisis. Or just imagine a bright light of healing warming your lower back that now aches from (still!) standing behind the guy with the truckload of frozen dinners. (While you're at it, send some healing light to his gastrointestinal system.)

When you have connected with your Holy Self, your time is always yours—and blessed with the backing of the Universe—even when you're in the company of others.

The Youest You

Make a commitment right now to honor your Self with a regular solitude practice. Think of your own first name. Let it be a symbol, as all names are, for your unique being. Even though thousands or even millions of people might share that name, only you will invest it with the singularity of your divine personality. Then:

- Take a 3 x 5 card and write the following on it: *I celebrate my* [First Name]*-ness. I will be the* [First Name]*-est* [First Name] *I can be. Thank you, Universe!* (For example: I celebrate my Davidness. I will be the Davidest David I can be. Thank you, Universe!)

- Read the card out loud. You may even wish to begin and end each alone time with these words to set the intention of your practice as well as your return to outward life.

By all means, add your own affirmations to the card. Whatever inspiring, loving words give you joy, write them down and declare them with pride.

All This is Yours

Resurfacing

There is nothing like returning to a place that remains unchanged to find the ways in which you yourself have altered.
—Nelson Mandela

Once you get the hang of your solitude practice, you may find there's a dangerous side effect: You want to remain alone for longer and longer periods of time. Moreover, you might actually resent returning to the "real world" of others.

No doubt finding our true selves is much like discovering a soul mate. The impetus is to hole up and enjoy each other for a while. There is a delicious pull toward solitude. I know; that pull has been instrumental in the demise of a few of my relationships. Paradoxically, solitude can make a relationship healthier while potentially threatening it. Whenever possible, we must share the gifts we receive during our practice—the boon of our revitalized souls—so that solitude might be released from its threatening nature.

It is our responsibility to find out exactly what we need to

> **Solitude is not hermitage.**

refuel, but not to retain. Energy is created in order to be spent. Solitude is not hermitage. Being part of community is essential to our health as balanced human beings. What matters is that when we resurface, we honor the presence of our Holy Self. That Self becomes a shield from societal pressure to assimilate blindly, from over-extending our energies in the name of love. Our Holy Selves should be an oasis of joy that we—as well as beloved others—drink from and belly-flop into.

Don't fear loving yourself too much. As far as I know, no one has ever died from too much love. Instead, what happens goes something like this: We recognize ourselves as sparks of Creation and love ourselves as we love that Great Mystery. We become so full of the joy love gives that it pours out of us—radiates—to others. Most of us have been in the presence of a blissfully centered person who seems to exude positivity. Most often, being around someone like that raises our own levels of happiness, even hope for mankind. It's the same as when we stand in front of a fine work of art; we are moved. Its beauty brings out the beauty in us. This is what we do when we practice solitude. We create the work of art that touches and inspires others to be their best selves as well.

So return, re-emerge, resurface. Bring your gifts back with you to share.

The Rewards of a Solitary Life

I want to be with those who know secret things
or else alone.
—Rainer Maria Rilke

The times in my life that I have been most unhappy were the times that I was not paying attention to my inner life of solitude. My Holy Self was lost to the outer world's busyness of following the crowd, doing for others without a thought for myself besides getting showered and dressed and fed. When a major break-up of a long-time romance and the death of my father hurled me into concentrated solitude, I resisted that life, even though I'd been comfortable with being alone my whole life. By my thirties, I'd bought into society's belief that solitude is suspect. Sure, a few moments alone to gather your thoughts is acceptable, but extended periods of time by yourself typically indicated that something was wrong with you. It took a few years for the message to sink in that there was nothing wrong with me. In fact, I had more energy than I ever had. When I chose to be social, I was more present. And, amazingly, I no longer got peeved while waiting in line at the Post Office.

Regular sessions of solitude help us to become noble, peaceful human beings. Solitude also offers the blessing of allowing us to recharge our souls' batteries so that we have not only more energy to devote to others, but more *honest* energy.

After reading this book, you may have mixed feelings about beginning a solitude practice. Perhaps it has made you excited. Or maybe the concept still seems like a far-fetched venture. If you're still questioning the validity of solitude, remember that the time you devote to discovering and honoring your Holy Self is an investment in the happiness of your friends and family. It is also an expression of gratitude to the Divine Energy that created you. Above all, it is a reunion of Self and Spirit.

A person who embraces the Holy Self:

- is a better listener
- exudes warmth
- is more helpful to family and friends
- has more energy
- is playful

- retains peacefulness in stressful situations
- is more fun on dates
- feels compassion toward strangers
- can fly

Okay, that last one isn't true, but it can feel like that sometimes. Taking regular alone time for yourself is a simple way to empower yourself, and let that power wash over your other relationships whether they're with people you know or complete strangers.

Strangers? Really? Sure thing. To illustrate, I'll share this brief story: In the summer of 2003, I worked at the café my friends Bruce and Bob owned in order to earn some extra cash for an upcoming trip to India. One night, right before closing, a woman walked in with a scowl planted on her face. It had been a busy night and I was tired. My hair was a mess and my apron was slathered with coffee-infused milk foam and Panini condiments. I felt myself bristle as she approached the counter. In a low, harried voice, she asked for an herbal iced tea. We only had regular iced tea, and I told her this.

"Bob *always* makes me *herbal* iced tea," she snapped.

I nearly leapt over the counter and strangled her. But something made me stop and take a deep breath. Maybe, like me, she lived alone and was having a lonely day. Or maybe work was getting her down. Who knew?

"Tough day?" I asked.

Immediately, her face softened. "Yeah. You know..." She proceeded to tell me about the difficulties she was having with a next-door neighbor who objected to her friendly but very large Labrador Retriever.

I smiled and told her to choose the herbal tea she wanted; I'd make the iced tea for her. From that day on, she smiled whenever she saw me at the café or around the neighborhood. I won't pretend that she and I became friends after that encounter, but there's no doubt that good energy was created out of bad. That kind of thing heals the world.

I'm convinced my capacity to handle that sour situation with compassion came from the amount of time I spent alone, recharging my soul's batteries. Otherwise, I might have felt depleted of energy (having given it to customers all night) or even crabby about why she was being so inconsiderate toward a fellow human being who obviously looked like she, too, had had a rough day.

Poet and teacher Robert Bly tells a story about a young man who loses his sense of self. This young man had long hair, which he loved. It was his identity. One day, his parents sat him down in the middle of the kitchen and cut off all his hair, leaving the young man grieving for the loss his old self. The young man's grandfather entered the kitchen and, upon seeing his despondent grandson, said, "Come with me." He took the young man to the edge of the ocean. They stood there a while, staring out at its quiet magnificence. After a long time, the grandfather spoke. "All this," said the old man, his arm sweeping across the expanse of nature's beauty, "is yours."

If you begin to incorporate regular sessions of rejuvenative solitude into your life, and tend your soul with gentle kindness, all the world will be yours. It will no longer matter what others expect of you, because you will know and honor your deepest truth. You will live with joyful connection to all around you. You will fill your journal with stories about your vital, wild, goofy, fascinating journey to Self. Your friends and family will notice how peaceful you've become, and how genuinely present you are for them.

Most of all, you will have become the absolutely best human being you can be. That human being will support you and stand by you every day of your life, through glorious times and tragedies. Honor yourself with a just few minutes of solitude a day, and you will find that something magnificent has happened: You have become your own best friend. Your Holy Self.

Acknowledgements

Eternal thanks to all my teachers—family, friends, students, clients, mentors, and helping spirits in all worlds.

42003853R00081

Made in the USA
Charleston, SC
14 May 2015